Franz Joseph Haydn

Die Schöpfung
The Creation

VOCAL SCORE

Edited by

A. PETER BROWN
with
JULIE SCHNEPEL

Music Department
OXFORD UNIVERSITY PRESS
Oxford and New York

Oxford University Press, Walton Street, Oxford OX2 6DP, England

Oxford University Press, 200 Madison Avenue, New York, NY 10016, USA

Oxford is a trade mark of Oxford University Press

The full score is also on sale. Full scores, vocal scores, and instrumental parts
are available for hire from the publisher's hire library.
Scoring: 3 flutes, 2 oboes, 2 clarinets, 2 bassoons, contrabassoon, 2 horns, 2 trumpets, 3 trombones,
timpani, strings, continuo; soprano, alto, tenor, and bass soloists, and chorus.

Duration: *c.*1 hour 40 minutes

CONTENTS

Kurt Berentsen

PREFACE

Next to Handel's *Messiah*, Haydn's *The Creation* is perhaps the most frequently performed oratorio. Within several years of its first public Viennese performance in March of 1799 *The Creation* was heard in all the major European centres from London to Moscow,[1] and during Haydn's lifetime this oratorio became the first universally acknowledged musical masterpiece with unpredictable speed. After its popularity went into eclipse during the nineteenth century, it re-emerged once again into public favour. In part, this was stimulated by the appearance of Mandyczewski's edition for the Breitkopf & Härtel *Gesamtausgabe* in 1922 and by the post-World War II renaissance in Haydn scholarship and performance. Yet despite the recovery of important sources that provide much new information about how the piece was performed, none of this has been incorporated into any available edition; it is the purpose of this publication to fill this void.

Mandyczewski's text was based on Haydn's self-published first edition in full score, with both German and English texts, which appeared in late February 1800. Mandyczewski added a few expressive indications, supplemented the articulation markings, and printed only the German text. In contrast, the present edition is based on authentic sets of parts and scores from the Tonkünstler Societät (sources **A** and **D**), Haydn's Estate (**B** and **E**), an incomplete set of orchestral parts from the Gesellschaft der Musikfreunde in Vienna (**C**), the engraver's score for the first edition (**F1**), and the first edition itself (**F2**), as well as the libretto for the first performances in 1798. The resulting text has been further emendated in order to bring simultaneous and parallel passages into conformity when justified. A full description of the sources and important variants among them are noted in the editors' report, which is published with the full score.

Since the publication of the first edition with both English and German texts, the English has come under fire. Later criticism was based in part on a misunderstanding of its history: the English text was believed to have been retranslated from the German, rather than being the original version which Haydn had acquired sometime during his second London residence. This old belief provided the justification for 'improving' the English text in editions still in use, dating from Vincent Novello's (1847) to Robert Shaw's (1957). In fact, Haydn composed his music for the German translation, which had been arranged and translated by the Baron Gottfried van Swieten, who then set the original English to Haydn's music.[2] In 1988 Nicholas Temperley attempted to do 'Swieten's task over again',[3] which resulted in a recomposition of portions of Haydn's music and a modernization of the syntax in order to make the English fit the music better. Again, the English text as Haydn authorized it has been disturbed. Needless to say, such activity could also be justified for Handel's oratorios, since it could be argued that his English declamation, when compared to that of Purcell and Britten, also leaves something to be desired. But in either case such improvements ultimately lose more for their composers than they gain for today's audiences. Therefore, it is our belief that van Swieten's underlay of the English text, as approved by the composer, is the only acceptable version. Thus, we offer the English text and its music as Haydn intended it, as revealed in **E**, **F1**, and **F2**; this allows both singers and conductors the opportunity to judge and then retain

or alter words or phrases according to their own style of declamation. Spelling in both the German and English has been modernized, whilst Haydn's syllabification and punctuation have been generally maintained, modified only as absolutely necessary for present-day use. Broken slurs have been added without comment to clarify the underlay of the English in contradistinction to the German text, though Haydn's own slurs have been left intact.

This edition, unlike any other available, allows for the many options of eighteenth-century practice. During Haydn's lifetime, *The Creation* was performed in every imaginable venue, from renditions in the chamber atmosphere of private salons to those in Vienna's Burgtheatre in which *c.*200 performers participated.[4] Whilst our edition does not and cannot account for such *ad hoc* salon performances, it is the first to account for the many public renditions that Haydn himself conducted using large forces. On these occasions, the orchestra consisted of *c.*120 players, which included doubled trumpets, timpani, and trombones, as well as three wind bands consisting of pairs of flutes, oboes, clarinets, bassoons, and horns, as well as a single contrabassoon, and a string body comparable to that of today's modern symphony orchestra. In the full score and orchestral material, we have attempted, on the basis of solo/tutti markings in the parts from which Haydn conducted, to determine how the activities of these groups were distributed: it seems that all players participated in the choruses and some of the dramatic and pictorial moments in the accompanied recitatives, and reduced forces were used for the arias, some of the remaining recitatives, and 'orchestral' pieces. For those using smaller orchestras, our text will also aid in decisions as to where single as opposed to double winds might be used. For performances with one player on each of the wind and timpani parts, all would play throughout.

We also know something about how these large forces were distributed, from a report by Johan Berwald (1758–1825), the uncle of the Swedish composer Franz Berwald, who was in the audience of the Burgtheatre on 19 March 1799: 'When we entered, we saw that the stage proper was set up in the form of an amphitheatre. Down below at the fortepiano sat Kapellmeister Weigl, surrounded by the vocal soloists, the chorus, a violoncello, and a double bass. At one level higher stood Haydn himself with the conductor's baton. One level higher than this on one side were the first violins, led by Paul Wranitzky, and on the other the second violins, led by his brother Anton Wranitzky. In the centre: violas and double basses [*sic*; cellos?]. In the wings, more double basses; on higher levels the wind instruments, and at the very top: trumpets, kettledrums, and trombones.'[5] Such a set-up, with the chorus placed in front of the orchestra, also works well using small forces when the ratio of orchestral players to singers is two to one. When the size of the chorus is more equal to (or greater than) that of the orchestra, the placement of the chorus behind the orchestra might be more advantageous.

Haydn always used three soloists: soprano (Gabriel and Eve), tenor (Uriel), and bass (Raphael and Adam);[6] many recent performances use five, which, apart from underlining the dramatic distinction of new characters with new voices, also solves the problem of the final chorus, which requires an additional alto soloist. These few bars could easily be negotiated by the soprano who sang Gabriel. When only three soloists are used, an agile alto from the chorus should complete the quartet.

According to Haydn's biographer Giuseppe Carpani, the solo parts should 'be executed with simplicity, exactness, expression, and deportment, but without ornaments.'[7] Haydn told Albert Christoph Dies, concerning the March 1808 performance at which the composer made his last public appearance, that the soprano Demoiselle Fischer 'sang her part with the greatest delicacy, and so accurately that she did not permit herself the least unsuitable addition,' by which, according to Dies, Haydn 'meant cadenzas, ornaments, *Eingänge*, and so on.'[8] Though one cannot take Carpani's declaration and Dies's gloss at face value, the impression is that Haydn wished for few but appropriate additions.

The authenticity of the ornaments in the vocal parts owned by Haydn and the Tonkünstler Societät are questionable. Nevertheless, they are often beautiful and deserving of consideration. Many of the ornaments embellish fermatas and one can hardly believe that Haydn would object to the small cadenzas added by the solo singers or the modest addition of trills and turns to enhance the melody. For those who would like examples or models to emulate, these embellishments, if not provably authentic, at least conform to Haydn's guidelines. Unexpectedly, the Tonkünstler Societät's embellishments (A) seem less worthy than those from Haydn's Estate. Among the Estate material (B), perhaps the most controversial embellishments are those found in Eve's part for the longest of the *secco* recitatives (No. 29). But this is her last opportunity to sing alone; it is possibly the only time the embellishments exceed the elderly Haydn's preferred restraint.

We have included variants and additions from the solo vocal parts of sources A and B that are not in the first edition in footnotes. The performer, however, should realize that A was used in Vienna at least until the end of the nineteenth century, and that its ornaments probably post-date Haydn. Nevertheless, we have included them since they tell us something of where additions might be placed. The editors consider the ornaments and embellishments in B to be of particular value; these should be seriously considered for inclusion in Gabriel's two arias (Nos. 9 and 16).

Haydn mainly used four sign ornaments: *tr* , $\sim$, ∞ , and the so-called 'Haydn' ornament or, as he called it, a 'half mordent' (∞ or $\sim$). The latter has been traditionally rendered as ᵗᵗ or ᵗᵗ depending on tempo and context. Even though Haydn (in his letters of 20 July 1781 and 10 December 1785) took his publisher Artaria to task for not clearly differentiating between the four signs,[9] *The Creation*'s authentic scores and parts are often unclear as to which sign is meant; in this edition we have retained the reading of the sources. By the late 1790s, the distinctions between ∞ and ∞ were perhaps all but obliterated and the context rather than the sign itself seems to determine the realization. The former sign is used most frequently; the latter is found only in No. 24, b. 38. Sometimes Haydn uses a sign to continue an ornament that is already written out; in these instances we have substituted the full notation. Finally, we have retained Haydn's notation of the appoggiatura, which is performed as half the value of the main note, but with the auxiliary note notated as taking a value no less than a semiquaver. Variants and inconsistencies among and within the sources are documented in the editors' report in the full score.

In performing the narrative of the recitatives, the soloists should inform themselves as to the addition of appoggiaturas and the treatment of cadential dissonance. Since such decisions involve individual declamatory style, and depend on whether English or German is the performed language, this edition contains only the appoggiaturas and cadential dissonances found in or added to the sources.[10]

When Haydn conducted his oratorio, both Beda Plank, a Kremsmünster monk, and Griesinger commented on his tempos: the former thought the pace more moderate than that to which he was accustomed; the latter implied something livelier when he commented that Haydn 'conducted with youthful fire.'[11] Though documentation is lacking for the tempos of specific numbers, Haydn's own interpretation for 26 December 1802 was advertised as two hours long.[12] Compared to many current performances, Haydn's must have been a fast-paced one (*c*.100 min.) if an intermission or the customary concerto performance took place between two of the parts and no cuts were made.

The keyboard reduction in this edition is by the Leipzig Cantor, A. E. Müller, and was first printed by Breitkopf & Härtel in 1800. Of this arrangement, Haydn said that it was 'the best, most idiomatic [*verständlichsten*], and the easiest of all its brothers.'[13] Müller does not attempt to account for every note in the orchestral score, but presents a version appropriate to the limitations of the keyboard. Haydn concurred with this approach, as evidenced by the corrections he made to Müller's keyboard version for the vocal score of *The Seasons*.[14] We have modified Müller's text to conform to the orchestral score in dynamics, articulation, and so forth without comment.

The editors' report, full details of sources and editorial method, and a bibliography can be found in the full score.

A. Peter Brown
Julie Schnepel

NOTES

[1] The first six performances were private ones that took place at the Schwarzenberg Palais in Vienna (29, 30 April and 7, 10 May 1798; 2, 4 March 1799). The first public performance was on 19 March 1799 at the Burgtheatre.

[2] See Nicholas Temperley, 'New Light on the Libretto of *The Creation*' in *Music in Eighteenth-Century England. Essays in Memory of Charles Cudworth*, ed. Christopher Hogwood and Richard Luckett (Cambridge: Cambridge University Press, 1983).

[3] See Franz Joseph Haydn, *The Creation*, ed. Nicholas Temperley (London: Peters, 1988).

[4] See A. Peter Brown, *Performing Haydn's* The Creation: *Reconstructing the Earliest Renditions* (Bloomington: Indiana University Press, 1986), pp. 2–7.

[5] See C. G. Stellan Mörner, 'Haydniana aus Schweden um 1800' in *Haydn-Studien* II (1969), pp. 5–8.

[6] See Brown, *Performing*, pp. 2–7.

[7] Giuseppe Carpani, *Le Haydine* (Milan: Bussinelli, 1812), p. 182.

[8] Albert Christoph Dies, *Biographische Nachrichten von Joseph Haydn* (Vienna: Camesinaische Buchhandlung, 1810); modern ed. by Horst Seeger (Berlin: Henschelverlag, 1959), p. 167.

[9] See H. C. Robbins Landon, *The Creation and The Seasons: The Complete Authentic Sources for the Word-Books* (Cardiff: University College Cardiff Press, 1985), pp. 448–9, 674–5.

[10] For guidance in this and related areas, see Frederick Neumann, *Ornamentation in Baroque and Post-Baroque Music: With Special Emphasis on J. S. Bach*, and *Ornamentation and*

Improvisation in Mozart (Princeton: Princeton University Press, 1978 and 1986 respectively).

[11] According to Plank's diaries (published in Altmann Kellner, *Musikgeschichte des Stiftes Kremsmünster* [Kassel: Bärenreiter, 1956], pp. 567–8) and Griesinger's letter of 21 January 1801 (see Otto Biba, '*Eben komme ich von Haydn . . .*' *Georg August Griesingers Korrespondenz mit Joseph Haydns Verleger Breitkopf &: Härtel* [Zurich: Atlantis, 1987], p. 53.

[12] See the *Wiener Zeitung*, 14 September 1796 (p. 2647) and 18 December 1802 (p. 4557).

[13] Hermann von Hase, *Joseph Haydn und Breitkopf & Härtel* (Leipzig: Breitkopf & Härtel, 1909), p. 13.

[14] See Georg Feder, 'Haydns Korrekturen zum Klavierauszug der "Jahreszeiten"' in *Festschrift Georg von Dadelsen zum 60. Geburtstag*, ed. Thomas Kohlhase and Volker Scherliess (Neuhausen: Hanssler, 1978).

VORWORT

Neben Händels *Messias* ist Haydns *Die Schöpfung* vielleicht das Oratorium, welches am häufigsten aufgeführt wird. Innerhalb weniger Jahre nach der ersten öffentlichen Aufführung im März 1799 in Wien war *Die Schöpfung* in allen wichtigen europäischen Zentren von London bis Moskau zu hören,[1] und noch zu Lebzeiten Haydns wurde das Oratorium überraschend schnell zum ersten allgemein anerkannten musikalischen Meisterwerk. Im 19. Jahrhundert sank dann seine Popularität auf einen Tiefpunkt, anschließend aber eroberte es sich die öffentliche Gunst zurück. Diese Entwicklung wurde zum Teil durch das Erscheinen von Mandyczewskis Edition für die Gesamtausgabe von Breitkopf & Härtel im Jahre 1922 angeregt, sowie durch die Renaissance, welche die Haydn-Forschung und die Aufführung der Werke Haydns nach dem Zweiten Weltkrieg erlebte. Trotz der Wiederentdeckung wichtiger Quellen, die viele neue Informationen über die damalige Aufführungspraxis des Werkes brachten, sind diese neuen Erkenntnisse nicht in die zur Zeit erhältlichen Ausgaben eingeflossen. Es ist das Ziel der vorliegenden Edition, diese Lücke zu füllen.

Mandyczewskis Text basierte auf der ersten Ausgabe der Partitur, die Haydn mit sowohl deutschem als auch englischem Text selbst herausbrachte und die im späten Februar des Jahres 1800 erschien. Mandyczewski fügte einige Ausdrucksbezeichnungen hinzu, ergänzte Artikulationsangaben und druckte lediglich den deutschen Text. Im Gegensatz dazu stützt sich die vorliegende Edition auf authentische Stimmen und Partituren der Tonkünstler Societät (Quellen **A** und **D**), Haydns Nachlaß (**B** und **E**), einen unvollständigen Satz Orchesterstimmen der Gesellschaft der Musikfreunde in Wien (**C**), die Partiturvorlage des Notenstechers der ersten Ausgabe (**F1**) und auf die erste Ausgabe selbst (**F2**) sowie das Libretto der ersten Aufführungen im Jahre 1798. Der resultierende Text wurde weiter berichtigt, um synchron verlaufende und sich entsprechende Passagen zu vereinheitlichen, soweit dies gerechtfertigt schien. Eine ausführliche Beschreibung der Quellen und wichtigen Abweichungen zwischen ihnen enthält der Editionsbericht in der Partitur.

Seit der Veröffentlichung der ersten Ausgabe mit sowohl englischem als auch deutschem Text ist der englische Text ins Kreuzfeuer geraten. Spätere Kritik beruhte zum Teil auf einem Mißverständnis seiner Geschichte: Man glaubte, der englische Text sei aus dem Deutschen übersetzt worden, während in Wahrheit dieser die Originalfassung darstellte, in deren Besitz Haydn während seines zweiten Londoner Aufenthalts gekommen war. Diese alte Annahme rechtfertigte „Verbesserungen" des englischen Texts in Ausgaben, von denen noch heute Gebrauch gemacht wird und die in die Zeit zwischen Vincent Novellos (1847) und Robert Shaws (1957) zu datieren sind. Tatsächlich komponierte Haydn seine Musik für eine deutsche Übersetzung aus dem Englischen, die Baron Gottfried van Swieten angefertigt und eingerichtet hatte. Anschließend unterlegte van Swieten Haydns Komposition mit dem originalen englischen Text.[2] Im Jahre 1988 unternahm Nicholas Temperley den erneuten Versuch, van Swietens Aufgabe zu bewältigen,[3] was zu einer Neukomposition von Teilen der Musik Haydns sowie einer Modernisierung der Syntax führte, mit dem Ziel, das Englische der Musik besser anzupassen. Wieder wurde der englische Text, so wie Haydn ihn für gut befunden hatte,

verändert. Es erübrigt sich festzustellen, daß man bei einer solchen Betrachtung ein entsprechendes Verfahren auch bei Händels Oratorien rechtfertigen könnte; denn es ließe sich ja argumentieren, daß Händels Umgang mit der englischen Sprache verglichen mit dem Purcells und Brittens einiges zu wünschen übrig läßt. In jedem Falle schaden solche Verbesserungen letztendlich mehr den Komponisten, als daß sie heutigen Hörern nützen. Deshalb sind wir der Meinung, daß van Swietens Unterlegung des englischen Texts, die ja die Zustimmung des Komponisten fand, die einzig akzeptable Fassung darstellt. So präsentieren wir den englischen Text und die Musik, wie es Haydn beabsichtigte und die Quellen **E**, **F1** und **F2** es belegen. Dies gibt sowohl Sängern als auch Dirigenten die Möglichkeit, sich ihr eigenes Urteil zu bilden, Worte und Phrasen zu übernehmen oder entsprechend den Erfordernissen des persönlichen Vortragsstils abzuwandeln. Sowohl der deutsche als auch der englische Text erscheinen in moderner Orthographie. Haydns Silbentrennung und Zeichensetzung jedoch wurden weitgehend unverändert übernommen und lediglich dann modifiziert, wenn es absolut unumgänglich für den heutigen Sprachgebrauch erschien. Gestrichelte Bindebögen wurden kommentarlos ergänzt, um die Unterlegung des englischen Texts—im Unterschied zum deutschen—zu verdeutlichen, wobei Haydns eigene Bindebögen jedoch unangetastet blieben.

Im Gegensatz zu allen anderen zur Zeit erhältlichen Ausgaben berücksichtigt die vorliegende die vielen Formen der Aufführungspraxis des 18. Jahrhunderts. Zu Lebzeiten Haydns wurde *Die Schöpfung* in jedem erdenklichen Konzertraum aufgeführt, von der Wiedergabe in der Kammermusik-Atmosphäre privater Salons bis zu den Aufführungen im Burgtheater Wiens, an denen etwa 200 Musiker mitwirkten.[4] Während unsere Ausgabe der Vielzahl der *ad hoc* Salon-Aufführungen nicht Rechnung trägt und nicht tragen kann, ist sie die erste Edition, die die vielen öffentlichen Wiedergaben des Werkes, die Haydn selbst unter Einsatz großer Orchester- und Chorstärken dirigierte, berücksichtigt. Bei diesen Gelegenheiten bestand das Orchester aus etwa 120 Musikern einschließlich doppelt besetzter Trompeten, Pauken und Posaunen sowie dreier Bläsergruppen, die sich aus doppelt besetzten Flöten, Oboen, Klarinetten, Fagotten und Hörnern sowie einem einzelnen Kontrafagott zusammensetzten. Die Besetzung der Streicher war mit der eines heutigen modernen Sinfonieorchesters vergleichbar. In der Dirigierpartitur und im Orchestermaterial haben wir den Versuch unternommen, auf der Basis der Solo/Tutti-Angaben in den Stimmen, die unter Haydns Dirigat verwendet wurden, zu ermitteln, wie diese Orchestergruppen eingesetzt wurden: Augenscheinlich beteiligte sich das gesamte Orchester an den Chorsätzen und an einigen dramatischen und programmatischen Abschnitten der Accompagnato-Rezitative. Reduzierte Besetzungen dagegen wurden in den Arien, den übrigen Rezitativen und den „orchestralen" Abschnitten verwendet. Dirigenten, denen kleinere Orchester zur Verfügung stehen, wird unsere Ausgabe die Entscheidung erleichtern, wo einfach besetzte Bläser im Gegensatz zu doppelt besetzten eingesetzt werden können. Bei Aufführungen mit nur einem Spieler für jede Bläser- und Paukenstimme werden alle durchgehend eingesetzt.

Aus einem Bericht Johan Berwalds (1758—1825), der sich im Publikum des Burgtheaters am 19. März 1799 befand und der

der Onkel des schwedischen Komponisten Franz Berwald war, wissen wir etwas darüber, wie diese großen Besetzungen verteilt waren: „Als wir eintraten, sahen wir, daß das eigentliche Theater in einer amphitheatralischen Form gebaut war. Unten am Fortepiano saß der Kapellmeister Weigl, von den Solosängern, dem Chor, einem Violoncello und einem Kontrabaß umgeben. Eine Stufe höher stand Haydn selbst mit dem Anführerstab. Noch eine Stufe höher standen auf der einen Seite: die Primo Violinen, von Paul Wranitzky angeführt, und auf der anderen: die 2do Violinen, von dessen Bruder Anton angeführt. Im Zentrum: Bratschen und Bässe. An den Flügeln ebenso Bässe; auf den höheren Stufen die Bläser, und zuletzt in der Höhe: Trompeten, Pauken und Posaunen."[5] Eine solche Aufstellung, bei der sich der Chor vor dem Orchester befindet, kann auch gut bei kleineren Besetzungen angewendet werden, wenn das Verhältnis zwischen Instrumentalisten und Sängern zwei zu eins ist. Kommt die Größe des Chores jedoch eher der des Orchesters gleich oder übertrifft diese noch, so ist die Aufstellung des Chores hinter dem Orchester vorteilhafter.

Haydn verwendete immer drei Solisten: einen Sopran (Gabriel und Eve), einen Tenor (Uriel) und einen Baß (Raphael und Adam).[6] Viele neuere Aufführungen werden mit fünf Solisten besetzt. Auf diese Weise wird nicht nur die dramatische Differenzierung zwischen den verschiedenen Charakteren mit Hilfe verschiedener Stimmen unterstrichen, sondern auch das Problem des Schlußchors, der eine zusätzliche Alt-Solostimme verlangt, gelöst. Diese wenigen Takte kann ohne weiteres der Sopran, der die Partie des Gabriel singt, bewältigen. Stehen jedoch nur drei Solisten zur Verfügung, so sollte eine flexible Altstimme aus dem Chor das Quartett vervollständigen.

Der Ansicht von Haydns Biographen Giuseppe Carpani zufolge sollten die Solo-Partien „mit Einfachheit, Genauigkeit, Ausdruck und Haltung, jedoch ohne Ornamente"[7] ausgeführt werden. Mit Bezug auf die Aufführung im März des Jahres 1808, bei der der Komponist zum letzten Mal öffentlich auftrat, sagte Haydn zu Albert Christoph Dies „zum Lobe der Demoiselle Fischer, sie hätte ihre Stimme mit der möglichsten Zierlichkeit und so treu gesungen, daß sie sich nicht den geringsten unzweckmäßigen Zusatz erlaubt hätte." Laut Dies bezog sich Haydn hier auf „Kadenzen, Ornamente, Eingänge usw.."[8] Obwohl man Carpanis Feststellung und Dies' Auslegung der Worte Haydns nicht verabsolutieren kann, besteht doch der Eindruck, daß Haydn wenige, aber angemessene Verzierungen wünschte.

Die Authentizität der Ornamente in den Vokalstimmen, die sich im Besitz Haydns und der Tonkünstler Societät befanden, ist fragwürdig. Trotzdem sind sie oft schön und verdienen Beachtung. Viele Ornamente verzieren Fermaten, und man kann sich kaum vorstellen, daß Haydn gegen die kleinen Kadenzen, welche die Solisten hinzufügten, und die bescheidene Ergänzung von Trillern und Doppelschlägen zur Intensivierung der Melodie Einwände erhoben hätte. Denjenigen, die Beispiele und Modelle nachahmen möchten, sei versichert, daß diese Verzierungen, auch wenn sie nicht nachgewiesenermaßen authentisch sind, doch mit Haydns Vorstellungen übereinstimmen. Überraschenderweise erscheinen die Ornamente der Tonkünstler Societät (**A**) weniger beachtenswert als die aus Haydns Nachlaß. Die vielleicht umstrittensten Verzierungen im Material des Nachlasses (**B**) befinden sich in Eves Part im längsten der *Secco-Rezitative* (Nr. 29). Es handelt sich jedoch um ihre letzte Gelegenheit, allein zu singen; es ist möglicherweise das einzige Mal, daß die Verzierungen über die vom älteren Haydn bevorzugte Zurückhaltung hinausgehen.

In den Fußnoten wird auf Varianten und Hinzufügungen in den solistischen Vokalstimmen der Quellen **A** und **B**, die sich nicht in der ersten Ausgabe befinden, hingewiesen. Der Interpret sollte sich jedoch darüber im klaren sein, daß Quelle **A** zumindest bis Ende des 19. Jahrhunderts in Wien in Gebrauch war und daß die Verzierungen vermutlich aus der Zeit nach Haydns Tod datieren. Dennoch haben wir die Ornamente übernommen, da sie Aufschluß darüber geben, wo Verzierungen angebracht werden könnten. Die Herausgeber messen den Verzierungen und Ornamenten in Quelle **B** besonderen Wert bei. Ihre Berücksichtigung bei der Wiedergabe der beiden Arien Gabriels (Nr. 9 und 16) sollte ernsthaft geprüft werden.

Im Wesentlichen benutzte Haydn vier Verzierungszeichen: *tr*, ᮊ, ∾, und die sogenannte „Haydn"—Verzierung oder, wie er selbst sagte, den „Halbmordent" (∾ oder ᮊ). Letzterer wird traditionell je nach Tempo und Kontext entweder als 𝄐 oder als 𝄐 ausgeführt. Obwohl Haydn seinen Verleger Artaria (in seinen Briefen vom 20. Juli 1781 und 10. Dezember 1785) wegen unzureichender Differenzierung zwischen den vier Symbolen ins Gebet nahm,[9] enthalten die authentischen Partituren und Stimmen der *Schöpfung* oft Unklarheiten darüber, welches Symbol gemeint ist. In der vorliegenden Edition wurde die Lesart der Quellen beibehalten. In den späten 90er Jahren des 18. Jahrhunderts waren die Unterschiede zwischen ∾ und ∾ vielleicht so gut wie verschwunden, und es war in erster Linie der Kontext—nicht das Zeichen selbst—, der die Ausführung des Ornaments bestimmte. Das erste der beiden Symbole wurde am häufigsten gebraucht; das Zweite ist nur in Nr. 24, Takt 38 zu finden. Manchmal benutzte Haydn ein Symbol, um eine Verzierung fortzuführen, die er bereits ausgeschrieben hatte. In diesen Fällen haben wir die vollständige Notation eingesetzt. Schließlich haben wir auch Haydns Notation der Appoggiatura beibehalten, die mit dem halben Notenwert der Hauptnote ausgeführt wird, wobei jedoch die Vorschlagsnote mindestens mit dem Wert einer Sechzehntelnote notiert wird. Abweichungen und Uneinheitlichkeiten zwischen den und innerhalb der Quellen sind im Editionsbericht der Partitur dokumentiert.

Für die Gestaltung der Rezitative sollten sich die Solisten über das Hinzufügen von Vorschlägen und die Behandlung kadenzieller Dissonanzen informieren. Da solche Entscheidungen vom individuellen Vortragsstil sowie von der Sprache, in der gesungen wird—Englisch oder Deutsch—, abhängen, enthält die vorliegende Ausgabe nur Vorschläge und kadenzielle Dissonanzen, die in den Quellen gefunden oder zu diesen hinzugefügt wurden.[10]

Als Haydn sein Oratorium dirigierte, äußerten sich sowohl Beda Plank, ein Mönch aus Kremsmünster, als auch Griesinger zu seinen Tempi: Ersterer empfand das Tempo als zurückhaltender als das, an welches er gewöhnt war, letzterer ließ durch seinen Kommentar, daß Haydn „mit jugendlichem Feuer"[11] dirigiert habe, auf eine lebhaftere Aufführung schließen. Obwohl Hinweise auf die Tempi spezifischer Nummern fehlen, war doch Haydns eigene Interpretation vom 26. Dezember 1802 mit einer Dauer von zwei Stunden angezeigt.[12] Verglichen mit heutigen Aufführungen muß Haydn ein relativ schnelles Tempo angeschlagen haben (etwa 100 Min.), falls es eine Pause gab oder die übliche Aufführung eines Solokonzerts zwischen den beiden Teilen stattfand und keine Kürzungen vorgenommen wurden.

Der Klavierauszug dieser Ausgabe stammt von dem Leipziger

Kantor A. E. Müller und wurde erstmalig von Breitkopf & Härtel im Jahre 1800 veröffentlicht. Haydn hielt ihn „für den besten, verständlichsten und leichtesten unter seinen Brüdern."[13] Müller hat nicht den Versuch unternommen, jede Note der Orchesterpartitur zu berücksichtigen, sondern präsentiert eine Version, die den Begrenzungen des Klaviers Rechnung trägt. Haydn stimmte diesem Ansatz zu, wie aus den Korrekturen hervorgeht, die er im Klavierpart von Müllers Klavierauszug der *Jahreszeiten* anbrachte.[14] Wir haben Müllers Notentext ohne Kommentar modifiziert, um ihn der Orchesterpartitur im Hinblick auf Dynamik, Artikulation usw. anzupassen.

Editionsbericht, vollständige Angaben zu Quellen und Editionsmethode sowie eine Bibliographie befinden sich in der Partitur.

Übersetzung: Petra Woodfull-Harris

A. Peter Brown
Julie Schnepel

NOTEN

[1] Die ersten sechs Aufführungen fanden in privatem Rahmen im Schwarzenberg Palais in Wien statt (29., 30. April und 7., 10. Mai 1798; 2., 4. März 1799). Die erste öffentliche Aufführung fand am 19. März 1799 im Burgtheater statt.

[2] Siehe: Nicholas Temperley, „New Light on the Libretto of The Creation" in *Music in Eighteenth-Century England. Essays in Memory of Charles Cudworth*, Hrsg. Christopher Hogwood und Richard Luckett (Cambridge: Cambridge University Press, 1983).

[3] Siehe: Franz Joseph Haydn, *The Creation*, Hrsg. Nicholas Temperley (London: Peters, 1988).

[4] Siehe: A. Peter Brown, *Performing Haydn's* The Creation: *Reconstructing the Earliest Renditions* (Bloomington: Indiana University Press, 1986), S. 2—7.

[5] Siehe: C. G. Stellan Mörner, „Haydniana aus Schweden um 1800" in *Haydn-Studien* II (1969), S. 5—8.

[6] Siehe: Brown, *Performing*, S. 2—7.

[7] Giuseppe Carpani, *Le Haydine* (Mailand: Bussinelli, 1812), S. 182.

[8] Albert Christoph Dies, *Biographische Nachrichten von Joseph Haydn* (Wien: Camesinaische Buchhandlung, 1810); moderne Ausgabe von Horst Seeger (Berlin: Henschelverlag, 1959), S. 167.

[9] Siehe: H. C. Robbins Landon, *The Creation and The Seasons: The Complete Authentic Sources for the Word-Books* (Cardiff: University College Cardiff Press, 1985), S. 448—449, 674—675.

[10] Im Hinblick auf Informationen über dieses und benachbarte Themengebiete siehe: Frederick Neumann, *Ornamentation in Baroque and Post-Baroque Music: With Special Emphasis on J. S. Bach*, und *Ornamentation and Improvisation in Mozart* (Princeton: Princeton University Press, 1978 bzw. 1986).

[11] Laut Planks Tagebüchern (erschienen in: Altmann Kellner, *Musikgeschichte des Stiftes Kremsmünster* [Kassel: Bärenreiter, 1956], S. 567—568) und Griesingers Brief vom 21. Januar 1801 (siehe: Otto Biba, „*Eben komme ich von Haydn...*" *Georg August Griesingers Korrespondenz mit Joseph Haydns Verleger Breitkopf & Härtel* [Zürich: Atlantis, 1987], S. 53).

[12] Siehe: die *Wiener Zeitung*, 14. September 1796 (S. 2647) und 18. Dezember 1802 (S. 4557).

[13] Hermann von Hase, *Joseph Haydn und Breitkopf & Härtel* (Leipzig: Breitkopf & Härtel, 1909), S. 13.

[14] Siehe: Georg Feder, „Haydns Korrekturen zum Klavierauszug der 'Jahreszeiten'" in *Festschrift Georg von Dadelsen zum 60. Geburtstag*, Hrsg. Thomas Kohlhase und Volker Scherliess (Neuhausen: Hänssler, 1978).

DIE SCHÖPFUNG · *THE CREATION*

Edited by A. Peter Brown
with Julie Schnepel

FRANZ JOSEPH HAYDN (1732–1809)
Piano reduction by August Eberhard Müller

Part 1

No. 1 Overture

Die Vorstellung des Chaos · *The Representation of Chaos*

Printed in Great Britain

OXFORD UNIVERSITY PRESS, MUSIC DEPARTMENT, WALTON STREET, OXFORD OX2 6DP
Photocopying this copyright material is ILLEGAL.

2

Scene 1

No. 2 Recitative (Raphael/Uriel) and Chorus

Im Anfange schuf Gott Himmel und Erde · *In the beginning God created the heaven and the earth.*

Und der Geist Gottes schwebte auf der Fläche der Wasser · *And the Spirit of God moved upon the face of the waters.*

¹ Added to **A**

The Creation

No. 3 Aria (Uriel) and Chorus

Nun schwanden vor dem heiligen Strahle · *Now vanish before the holy beams.*
Verzweiflung, Wut und Schrecken · *Despairing, cursing rage.*

14

The Creation

Scene 2

No. 4 Recitative (Raphael)

Und Gott machte das Firmament · *And God made the firmament*

Da tob-ten brau-send hef-ti-ge Stür-me;
Out-ra-geous storms now dread-ful a-rose;

wie Spreu vor dem
as chaff by the

Win-de, so flo-gen die Wol-ken.
winds are im-pel-led the clouds.

Die Luft durch-schnit-ten feu-ri-ge Blit-ze,
By hea-ven's fire the sky is en-fla-med,

The Creation

The Creation

Attacca

No. 5 Solo (Gabriel) with Chorus

Mit Staunen sieht das Wunderwerk · *The marv'llous work beholds amazed*

The Creation

Lob, das Lob des zwei - ten Tags.
God and of the se - cond day.
Mit Stau - -
The mar - -

Tags, das Lob des zwei - ten Tags.
God and of the se - cond day.

Tags, das Lob des zwei - ten Tags.
God and of the se - cond day.

Tags, das Lob des zwei - ten Tags.
God and of the se - cond day.

Tags, das Lob des zwei - ten Tags.
God and of the se - cond day.

p

- nen sieht das Wun - der-werk   der Him - mels - bür - ger fro - - he Schar,
- v'llous work be - holds a - maz'd   the glo - - rious hier - ar - chy of heav'n,

Und
And

Und
And

Und
And

Und
And

Und
And

f   *p*   *f*

¹Added(?) to **B**

Lob, das Lob des zwei - ten Tags.

The Creation

Scene 3

No. 6 Recitative (Raphael)

Und Gott sprach: Es sammle sich das Wasser · *And God said: Let the waters be gathered together*

RAPHAEL

Und Gott sprach: Es samm - le sich das Was - ser un - ter dem Him - mel zu - sam - men an

And God said: Let the wa - ters un - der the hea - ven be ga - ther - ed to - ge - ther un -

ei - nem Platz, und es er - schei - ne das trock - ne Land; und es ward so. Und Gott nann - te das trock - ne

- to one place, and let the dry land ap - pear; and it was so. And God call - ed the dry

Land: Er - de, und die Samm - lung der Was - ser nann - te er Meer; und Gott sah, dass es gut war.

land earth, and the ga - ther - ing of wa - ters call - ed he seas; and God saw that it was good.

[1] Performed

Land: Er - de,

The Creation

No. 7 Aria (Raphael)

Rollend in schäumenden Wellen · *Rolling in foaming billows*

The Creation

No. 8 Recitative (Gabriel)

Und Gott sprach: Es bringe die Erde Gras hervor · *And God said: Let the earth bring forth grass*

No. 9 Aria (Gabriel)

Nun beut die Flur das frische Grün · *With verdure clad the fields appear*

Nun beut___ die Flur das
With ver-dure clad the

fri-sche Grün dem Au-ge zur___ Er-göt-zung dar; den an-muts-vol-len Blick
fields ap-pear de-light-ful to___ the ra-vish'd sense; by flo-wers sweet and gay

er-höht___ der Blu-men sanf-ter Schmuck, er-höht_____ der___
en-han-ced is___ the charm-ing sight, en-han-----ced___

Blu-men sanf-ter Schmuck. Hier duf-ten Kräu-ter
is___ the charm-ing sight. Here vent___ their fumes the

¹ Turn only in **B**

The Creation

34

The Creation

The Creation

No. 10 Recitative (Uriel)

Und die himmlischen Heerscharen · *And the heavenly host proclaimed*

URIEL: Und die himm-li-schen Heer-scha-ren ver-kün-dig-ten den drit-ten
And the hea — ven — ly host pro-claim — ed the third

Tag, Gott prei — send und spre — chend:
day, prai — sing God and say — ing:

Attacca

No. 11 Chorus

Stimmt an die Saiten · *Awake the harp*

Vivace *f*

SOPRANO: Stimmt an die Sai-ten, er-greift die Lei-er! Lasst eu-ren Lob-ge-
A — wake the harp, — the lyre a-wake! — In shout and joy your

ALTO: Stimmt an die Sai-ten, er-greift die Lei-er! Lasst eu-ren Lob-ge-
A — wake the harp, — the lyre a-wake! — In shout and joy your

TENOR: Stimmt an die Sai-ten, er-greift die Lei-er! Lasst eu-ren Lob-ge-
A — wake the harp, — the lyre a-wake! — In shout and joy your

BASS: Stimmt an die Sai-ten, er-greift die Lei-er! Lasst eu-ren Lob-ge-
A — wake the harp, the lyre a-wake! — In shout and joy your

38

The Creation

The Creation

The Creation

42

The Creation

Scene 4

No. 12 Recitative (Uriel)

Und Gott sprach: Es sei'n Lichter an der Feste des Himmels · *And God said: Let there be lights in the firmament of heaven*

No. 13 Recitative (Uriel)

In vollem Glanze steiget jetzt die Sonne strahlend auf · *In splendour bright the sun is rising now*

No. 14 Trio and Chorus

Die Himmel erzählen die Ehre Gottes · *The heavens are telling the glory of God*

The Creation

The Creation

Part 2

Scene 1

No. 15   Recitative (Gabriel)

Und Gott sprach: Es bringe das Wasser · *And God said: Let the waters bring forth*

No. 16 Aria (Gabriel)

Auf starkem Fittiche schwinget · *On mighty pens uplifted soars*

GABRIEL

Auf star - - kem Fit - - ti-che
On might - - y pens up -

schwin-get sich der Ad - ler stolz, der Ad - ler_ stolz, und_ tei - - let die Luft im
- lift - ed soars the_ ea - gle a - loft, the ea - gle a - loft, and_ cleaves the sky in

schnel - le - sten_ Flu - - ge zur Son - - ne hin, zur
swift - est flight,_ in_ swift - est flight to the bla - - zing sun, to the

¹ Added to **B**

stolz,_____ und_____

The Creation

62

¹Added to **B**

²Turn only in **B**

The Creation

[1] Turn only in **B**   [2] Ornament on first and third beats in **A**, only on first in **B**   [3] Turn only in **B**   [4] Added(?) to **B**

No. 17 Recitative (Raphael)

Und Gott schuf grosse Walfische · *And God created great whales*

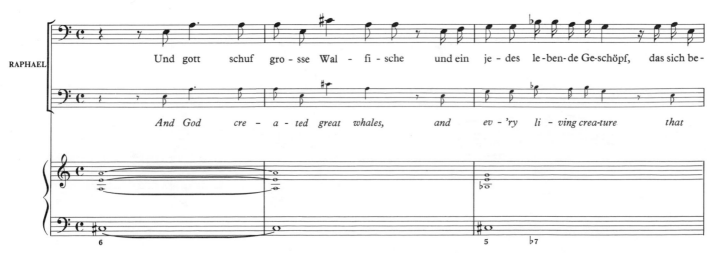

RAPHAEL

Und gott schuf gro - sse Wal - fi - sche und ein je - des le - ben- de Ge-schöpf, das sich be -

And God cre - a - ted great whales, and ev - 'ry li - ving crea-ture that

Poco Adagio
a tempo

-we-get, und Gott seg-ne-te sie, spre-chend: Seid frucht-bar al-le, meh-ret euch! Be-woh-ner der

mo-veth, and God bless-ed them, say-ing: Be fruit-ful all, and mul-ti-ply! Ye wing-ed

Luft, ver-meh-ret euch, und singt auf je-dem A - ste! Meh-ret euch, ihr Flu - ten-be-
tribes, be mul-ti-plied, and sing on ev-'ry tree! Mul-ti-ply, ye fin-ny

-woh-ner, und fül-let je-de Tie - fe! Seid frucht-bar, wach-set,
tribes, and fill each wat-'ry deep! Be fruit-ful, grow and

meh-ret euch! Er-freu-et euch in eu-rem Gott! Er-freu-et_euch in eu-rem Gott!
mul-ti-ply! And in your God and Lord re - joice! And in your God and Lord re - joice!

fz

¹ Additions to A

- we-get, und Gott seg-ne-te

The Creation

No. 18 Recitative (Raphael) *(ad lib.)*

Und die Engel rührten ihr' unsterblichen Harfen · *And the angels struck their immortal harps*

No. 19 Trio and Chorus

In holder Anmut steh'n · *Most beautiful appear*

The Creation

A

GABRIEL

In hol - der An - mut steh'n, mit jun - gem Grün ge - schmückt, die
Most beau - ti - ful ap - pear, with ver - dure young a - dorn'd the

wo - gig-ten Hü - gel da, die wo - gig-ten Hü - gel da. Aus
gen - tly slo - ping hills, the gen - tly slo - ping hills. Their

The Creation

74

The Creation

Attacca subito

The Creation

The Creation

The Creation

The Creation

The Creation

The Creation

The Creation

Scene 2

No. 20 Recitative (Raphael)

Und Gott sprach: Es bringe die Erde · *And God said: Let the earth bring forth*

RAPHAEL

¹Performed

Gat-tun-gen.

The Creation

No. 21 Recitative (Raphael)

Gleich öffnet sich der Erde Schoss · *Straight opening her fertile womb*

No. 22 Aria (Raphael)

Nun scheint in vollem Glanze · *Now heav'n in all her glory shone*

The Creation

No. 23 Recitative (Uriel)

Und Gott schuf den Menschen · *And God created man*

No. 24   Aria (Uriel)

Mit Würd' und Hoheit angetan · *In native worth and honour clad*

The Creation

The Creation

No. 25 Recitative (Raphael)

Und Gott sah jedes Ding · *And God saw everything*

No. 26 Chorus and Trio

Vollendet ist das grosse Werk · *Achieved is the glorious work*

The Creation

The Creation

The Creation

The Creation

Part 3

Scene 1

No. 27 Recitative (Uriel)

Aus Rosenwolken bricht · *In rosy mantle appears*

41

Seht das be-glück-te Paar, wie Hand in Hand es geht!
Be-hold the bliss-ful pair, where hand in hand they go!

46

Aus ih-ren Blik-ken strahlt des hei - ssen Danks Ge - fühl.
Their fla-ming looks ex - press what feels the grate - - ful heart.

51

Più moto

Bald singt in lau-tem Ton ihr Mund des Schöp-fers Lob.
A loud-er praise of God their lips shall ut - ter soon.

56

Lasst uns - 're Stim-me dann sich men - gen in ihr Lied!
Then let our voi-ces ring, u - ni - ted with their song!

¹ Added to A

Danks Ge - fühl.

The Creation

Scene 2

No. 28 Duet (Eva, Adam) with Chorus

Von deiner Güt', o Herr · *By thee with bliss O bounteous Lord*

The Creation

The Creation

The Creation

The Creation

The Creation

The Creation

The Creation

The Creation

The Creation

The Creation

The Creation

Scene 3

No. 29 Recitative (Adam, Eva)

Nun ist die erste Pflicht erfüllt · *Our duty we performed now*

No. 30 Duet (Adam, Eva)

Holde Gattin! Dir zur Seite · *Graceful consort! At thy side*

The Creation

The Creation

The Creation

dir sei es ganz ge - weiht.
thine, thine it whole shall be.

dir sei es ganz ge - weiht.
thine, thine it whole shall be.

Der tau - en - de
The dew drop - ping

Mor - gen, o wie er - mun - tert er!
morn, O how she quick - ens all!

Die Küh - le des A - bends, o wie er - quik - ket sie!
The cool - ness of ev'n, O how she all re - stores!

The Creation

The Creation

Final Scene

No. 31 Recitative (Uriel)

O glücklich Paar · *O happy pair*

[1] Salomon's performance libretto substitutes 'than' for 'as'.

The Creation

No. 32 Chorus

Singt dem Herren alle Stimmen · *Sing the Lord ye voices all*

The Creation

The Creation

The Creation

Processed and printed by
Halstan & Co. Ltd., Amersham, Bucks., England